Rookie Read-About® Science

All Along the River

WITHDRAWN

By Allan Fowler

Consultants:

Robert L. Hillerich, Professor Emeritus,
Bowling Green State University, Bowling Green, Ohio
Consultant, Pinellas County Schools, Florida

Lynne Kepler, Educational Consultant

Fay Robinson, Child Development Specialist

℗ CHILDRENS PRESS®
CHICAGO

Design by Beth Herman Design Associates

Library of Congress Cataloging-in-Publication Data

Fowler, Allan.
    All along the river / by Allan Fowler.
       p. cm. – (Rookie read-about science)
    ISBN 0-516-06019-8
    1. Rivers–Juvenile literature. [1. Rivers.] I. Title.
  II. Series: Fowler, Allan. Rookie read-about science.
GB1203.8.F69   1994
551.48'3–dc20   93-39646
                                                          CIP
                                                           AC

Where do rivers begin?

Some rivers begin as springs
rising out of the ground.

Others come from ponds
or lakes in the mountains.

Tiny streams flow
into small rivers...

which flow into bigger rivers,
and make them bigger still.

But the water in the rivers
once fell as rain...
or as snow that melted.

The rainwater runs downhill, gathers in rivers, and flows into the sea.

After heavy rains or
snowfalls, rivers
sometimes overflow.

Houses and fields, even
whole towns, are covered
by water.

This is called a flood.

People build large dams
to hold back the water.

Some dams use the
rushing water of rivers
to produce electricity.

Rapids develop where
a river runs swiftly,
often over rocks.

Many people think it's fun to "shoot the rapids" in a rubber raft.

A waterfall is a river tumbling over a cliff.

Niagara Falls, between the United States and Canada, is one of the biggest waterfalls in the world.

A swiftly flowing river
carries away soil and rocks.
Over a long period of
time, the land on each
side of the river wears away.

The river forms a valley.

The soil and rock that
rivers carry to the sea may
pile up and form new land.
The new land is called
a delta.

The city of New Orleans is on the delta of the Mississippi River.

Many important cities have grown up beside rivers.

People settled near rivers
because they provided
water to drink and fish
to eat.

The land near rivers is often rich and fertile – just right for farming.

And before there were any
cars and trains and planes...
people often went from one
place to another by traveling
in a boat on a river.

Cities, towns, and factories used to dump their waste into rivers. Some still do.

This pollutes the river's water. Polluted water is harmful to wildlife, plants, and people.

But now most people are more careful about keeping rivers clean.

You can enjoy a river
in many ways — fishing,
swimming, boating, or
exploring the wildlife
along its banks —

but only when the water is
clean...all along the river.

Words You Know

river

waterfall

lake

pond

spring

stream

valley

delta

rapids

flood

Index

About the Author

Allan Fowler is a free-lance writer with a background in advertising. Born in New York, he lives in Chicago now and enjoys traveling.

Photo Credits

North Wind Pictures – 4, 24, 31 (top left)

PhotoEdit – ©Tony Freeman, 6

Photri – 15, 16, 25; ©D. Trask, 17, 30 (top right)

©Carl Purcell – 21

SuperStock International, Inc. – ©Holton Collection, Cover; ©Christopher Harris, 11, 31 (bottom right); ©D.C. Lowe, 12; ©Hope Alexander, 26

Valan – ©J.R. Page, 3, 9; ©Lionel Bourque, 5, 30 (bottom left); ©Pam E. Hickman, 7, 30 (top left); ©François Morneau,8; ©Karen D. Rooney, 14, 31 (bottom left); ©Michel Julien, 18; ©Jean-Marie Jro, 19, 22, 31 (center left); ©Tom W. Parkin, 20, 31 (center right); ©V. Wilkinson, 23; ©J. Eascott/ Y. Momatiuk, 28; © Dr. A. Farquhar, 29, 31 (top right); ©J.A. Wilkinson, 30 (bottom right)

COVER: River